CAUGHT ON A CLIFF FACE

CAUGHT
ON A CLIFF FACE

Roger Schachtel

Illustrated by Charles Shaw

RAINTREE PUBLISHERS
Milwaukee • Toronto • Melbourne • London

Copyright © 1980, Raintree Publishers Inc.

All rights reserved. No part of this book may be reprod ʹced or utilized in any form or by any means, electronic or me ʰanical, including photocopying, recording, or by any information stoɪ... and retrieval system, without permission in writing from the Publisher. Inquiries should be addressed to Raintree Publishers Inc., 205 West Highland Avenue, Milwaukee, Wisconsin 53203.

Library of Congress Number: 79-21622

1 2 3 4 5 6 7 8 9 0 84 83 82 81 80

Printed and bound in the United States of America.

Library of Congress Cataloging in Publication Data

Schachtel, Roger.
  Caught on a Cliff Face.

  SUMMARY: Two men experience a stormy climb, become trapped on a ledge, and are subsequently rescued by helicopter from Badile Peak on the border between Italy and Switzerland.
    1. Mountaineering — Badile Peak — Juvenile literature.
2. Badile Peak — Description — Juvenile literature.
[1. Mountaineering. 2. Badile Peak] I. Shaw,
Charles, 1941-   II. Title.
GV199.44.B24S3   796.5ʹ22   79-21622
ISBN 0-8172-1560-3 lib. bdg.

CONTENTS

CHAPTER 1

Storm Clouds and Trouble

Philippe Berclaz and Philippe Héritier were hardly more than twenty years old. But they had been climbing mountains for many years. They were good at it. One day in August 1975, however, the two Philippes feared that they had climbed their last mountain.

The mountain is called the Piz Badile. It is in the Alps mountains in Switzerland. As mountains go, the Badile is not very high—10,853 feet to the top. But still, it is not an easy mountain to climb. The northeast side is like a wall and is 3,000 feet high. And Berclaz and Héritier planned to reach the top by climbing that wall. They would need all their mountain-climbing skills to make it.

The weather on August 22, 1975 was fine. There were no clouds in the sky. A person could see for miles. The temperature was like spring. On such a day it was hard for Berclaz and Héritier to think of the northeast face of the Badile as their enemy.

Berclaz and Héritier had spent the night before in a hut about halfway up the mountain. They hoped to reach the top of the Badile at least an hour before sundown on the day they started. Then they would go down by an easier and swifter route. The fine weather made them think that they could easily make it if they left early in the morning. On August 22 after a good night's sleep, they arose at 4:00 A.M. They left a few minutes later.

They had no way of knowing that they would be trapped on the cliff face longer than anyone who had tried to climb it before.

Berclaz and Héritier spent the next two hours crossing the small glacier—a sheet of ice and snow—that lies at the foot of the Badile's northeast wall. They reached the bottom of the rock face at 6:00 A.M. There they decided to leave behind most of the equipment they had brought.

The weather seemed too good. They would not need everything. They kept only the things they really needed to climb. There were ropes, hammers, and pitons. Pitons are large nails with eyes in them that a climber hammers into rock to attach a rope to. They also kept carabiners. These are the snaps used to connect a climbing rope to the eye of a piton. Finally, the two men decided to bring along their small gasoline stove. It weighed a little less than a pound. With the stove

they could treat themselves to some warm soup at the end of the day.

Each man carried a small rucksack on his back. The rucksacks held dry food, fruit, and extra clothing. For the first hour on the cliff, while it was still cool, the climbers wore their down-lined parkas. But as the sun warmed the cliff face, the parkas became unnecessary. Within an hour the men took them off and stuffed them in the rucksacks.

From far off, all the 3,000 feet of the northeast wall had looked the same to Berclaz and Héritier. It appeared as an unfriendly sheet of solid rock. There was no place for a hand or a foot of anyone crazy enough to want to climb the wall. But from close up, each part of the wall was different from the rest. The two Philippes would have to use different climbing skills for each part.

The best kind of mountain climbing is to be able to move as far as possible without using pitons and carabiners. In that way a person does not damage the mountain by hammering holes into it. Sometimes Berclaz and Héritier could move up the Badile one at a time, the full 130 feet of a rope without having to hammer in any additional pitons. But usually they had to use many pitons to be safe. One part was so hard to climb that they moved only sixty feet in one hour!

Much of the time, Berclaz and Héritier

climbed by belaying. This means that as one climbed, the other waited. Both were tied to one rope, and the rope was also fastened to pitons. One man climbed the length of the rope. When he had found a place to stop, he signaled his friend below. Then that one climbed to where the first climber awaited him. Then they would start all over again. The rope kept the men together. And because it was fastened to pitons, if the men slipped, they would not fall to the earth below. Instead, they would hang in the air from the rock face.

Berclaz and Héritier made good time. They stopped for a light lunch of fruit and dried meat on a tiny ledge halfway up the face. They took a half hour to eat and rest. They sat with their backs against the wall and hugged their knees. The view below was beautiful. They could see mountains and valleys. To the west lay the sparkling blue water of Lake Como.

The two climbers felt good. They were surprised, but not worried, when they saw storm clouds begin to gather. The weather report had said nothing about a storm or cloudy skies. So the two friends figured that the clouds would pass by as quickly as they had appeared. But the clouds did make the young men pack up and move ahead again.

The weather continued to worsen. At first

Berclaz and Héritier joked about the thick clouds. But soon they had to admit to themselves that they were no longer climbing just for fun. Now they knew that they *had* to reach the top well before sundown and start right back down. They did not have the proper equipment to camp out.

Suddenly rain began to fall. It beat against the rock face and the two climbers who clung to the rock. Then the rain stopped, and Berclaz and Héritier were glad. But if the temperature fell the rain would freeze as it hit. The rock face would become a sheet of ice.

Berclaz and Héritier couldn't believe what happened next. Snow began to fall! Soon they could see nothing but snow. They clung to the rock. It was not supposed to snow in August, but there it was. And if the snow continued, Berclaz and Héritier knew that they were in for real trouble.

CHAPTER 2

A Nest in the Storm

The weather did not clear. Instead, the snow fell more thickly as the minutes passed. And it stuck to the rock face. The surface was soon covered with a blanket of white. Not only did the continuing snowfall make it impossible for Berclaz and Héritier to see anything, the snow piling on the mountain's surface also made it impossible for them to think of continuing to climb. It would have been too much of a risk for one of them to serve as leader and move upward toward the top. He would almost certainly lose his footing on the wet, icy rock and be left dangling from the rock face. And how would the belayer down below save him?

Fortunately, Berclaz and Héritier were standing together on a tiny ledge. There was only enough space for them to stand beside each other. Yet this was much better than being separated by a rope length of 130 feet on different parts of the rock. Together, they could talk about their problem and decide what to do.

They decided that there was only one thing to do. They would look for a larger ledge where they could sit and wait for the storm to let up. And to do this they would have to move back down the face. One of them would belay the other down. If the one doing the looking lost his footing, then the belayer could use the rope that held them both to lift him back up.

The plan was dangerous. The belayer himself could lose his footing on the thin ledge. Then both men would be left dangling from the rock

face. But that was a risk they had to take. The ledge on which they were now standing was just too tiny for them to remain there.

Héritier would move down the wall while Berclaz remained on the ledge. When Héritier had discovered a more comfortable spot on the wall, he would signal his friend, who would climb down to join him. There they would wait out the storm.

Héritier's rope was fastened to a piton that was hammered into the rock. The same rope was also tied around Berclaz. As Héritier started to go down, he knew that this rope protected him from immediate danger. But not being able to see well worried him. So did the snow piling up. He had trouble finding handholds and footholds. And if there was a better spot for him and Berclaz to wait out the storm than where they had been standing, he couldn't see it.

Philippe Héritier moved slow inch by slow inch down the rock face. After an hour he had come almost to the end of the 130-foot rope. In the storm he felt alone. Only the rope between them told Héritier that he was with someone else. But when he reached the end of the rope and had still not found what he was looking for, he hardly knew what to do. Héritier pushed against the wall with his shoes so he could move a few feet to the right, then a few feet to the left.

As he moved to the left his legs struck a part of the rock that had been hidden by a pile of snow. Héritier kicked the snow away so he could see how much space was there.

The ledge was small, awfully small. Yet it was perhaps two square feet larger than the tiny lip of the rock he had been standing on with Berclaz. And there was no other place. This ledge would have to be their nest while the storm raged. Héritier believed it would be wide enough for them both to sit down on it.

He hammered a piton into the rock beside the ledge. Then he snapped a carabiner onto it. Next he passed the rope through the carabiner and tied it around himself. After sitting down on the ledge and making himself as comfortable as possible, he tugged on the rope three times. This signaled his friend to come down.

The tug on the rope was good news to Berclaz.

For the last hour he had felt just as cut off from Héritier as Héritier had from him. The falling snow had made it impossible to see Héritier a few moments after he had left the perch. Left by himself to wait, Berclaz had had little to do except worry. All he could think about was the falling snow that showed no sign of stopping.

Berclaz prepared to go down. He placed the two rucksacks on his back. He took the rope from the piton it was fastened to. Berclaz knew there was danger. His rope would be anchored only to the rock through a piton that Héritier had hammered into the mountain. It might be as far as 130 feet below. If Berclaz lost his footing and fell, he might drop 260 feet before the rope caught him and held him fast.

His fear did not improve Berclaz's performance as he began to move down the cliff face. With every step he worried about where the next handhold or foothold might be. The snow covered everything. Also, the cold froze his hands. His fingers did not quickly obey his brain's orders.

Berclaz found himself making the worst mistake a mountain climber can make. A climber should never push his body against the rock. Instead, he should lean slightly away from it. But without an anchor above him Berclaz did not believe he could do this. And fear was making him cling to the mountainside. Whenever he

found a handhold he held on tightly. And cling-
ing to the rock also weakened his footholds.

Then the worst happened. Berclaz had gone
about fifty feet when he lost his grip. At the same
moment, his feet were searching for a place to
plant themselves. He fell 200 feet before the rope
caught and held him. He was lucky that his head
and body did not strike the rock while he was
falling! Héritier saw his friend whiz past him. He
prayed that the fall would not break any bones
when the rope brought Berclaz up short.

a few hours, climbing would still be bad. They would still be trapped on their ledge. In two hours, night would fall. And climbing in the dark would be impossible, anyway.

But for the moment they had to continue as if there were no doubt of their survival. If they lost hope, if their spirits fell, then they would surely be lost.

They tried to make themselves as comfortable as possible. Unfortunately, the only way they could both sit on the ledge was by sitting half sideways, with their legs hanging over into empty space. They could not even face each other. And there wasn't room for the rucksacks on the ledge with them. They had to tie them to the same rope they were both attached to and let the sacks hang over the ledge.

The two had enough clothing on their bodies to make things far from hopeless. When the weather had begun to worsen, they had put on their down-filled parkas. These parkas were waterproofed and warm. The parkas also had hoods that protected the men's heads, necks, and faces. The hoods could be closed so that only the eyes and nose of the wearer could be seen. The men also had woolen hoods that fit tightly over their heads. The hoods had holes for eyes and noses. And they had mittens, and warm waterproof boots.

But Berclaz and Héritier knew they could not just sit there. They were doomed unless they found some way to exercise. The best protection from the cold is movement, but the ledge left little room to move. There wasn't even enough room for their feet. They spent their first hour together on the ledge doing exercises that would keep their blood moving, but wouldn't need much movement. They hit their hands and arms rapidly against their chests. They beat their fists against their legs and rubbed their legs. They took turns raising and lowering their arms 100 times.

They had to be careful that snow did not collect on the ledge. If it piled up, that would rob them of inches of space. They would find themselves sitting that much closer to the edge. The fact that the blinding storm prevented the two prisoners from looking far down didn't make them feel any safer. They could not forget that they might fall more than 2,000 feet if the piton that held them gave way and they lost their balance.

Because the climbers were trapped on the northeast face of the wall, darkness fell quickly for them. In the morning, of course, the sun would hit that side of the mountain first. But morning seemed far away. And if the snow continued into the morning, they would not see the sun.

The men thought of getting out their small

gasoline stove to make some hot soup. But they decided to wait until morning when the weather might be better. Then it would be easier to light the stove. Still, they needed food. Berclaz pulled up one of the rucksacks and took out some canned chicken, bacon bars, and fresh fruit. The food tasted wonderful. The danger the men faced seemed to make them very hungry.

As night came, the men felt very lonely. The white snow tore at them. Their little ledge seemed like a small life raft in the storm. They almost felt as if they had been buried alive.

Berclaz and Héritier had told several people where they planned to climb. So they knew that by now someone must have missed them. But

even if anyone knew what had happened, no one could look for them while the storm lasted. They felt sure, though, that as soon as the snow stopped falling, someone would set out to rescue them.

But even with the snow and cold, Berclaz and Héritier still found themselves getting sleepy. And they knew that if they both fell asleep, that might be the end. They would surely fall off the ledge. Yet at the same time, both needed to get some rest.

So the men worked out a plan. One would nod off for ten minutes or so. The other one would force himself to stay awake. He would keep the ledge free of snow and make sure that his dozing friend did not fall off the ledge. Then the other man would sleep. The plan didn't allow the men to rest very comfortably. Somehow, though, they both survived the night.

Unfortunately, so did the storm. In the morning it was still raging.

A Faint Sound and Joy

Even with the snow still falling, Berclaz and Héritier felt better and more hopeful in the morning. They had survived the night.

The cold had made their throats raw. But to awaken themselves, and as a way to exercise, they spent a few minutes shouting down the mountain. Maybe, they thought, somebody else was trapped somewhere down the mountain and might hear them. Then those persons might shout farther down into the valley. And maybe someone in the hut at the foot of the glacier would hear the second set of voices crying for help.

After shouting for a while Berclaz and Héritier decided to try to fix a warm meal. They pulled up one of the rucksacks and removed the small gasoline stove from inside it. Berclaz held the stove on his lap, for there was nowhere else to put it. Héritier tried to light the stove with a match. The wind blew out the small flame. Héritier tried again and again. Berclaz tried to help him. But each time Héritier lit a match, the wind blew it out.

Finally, after twenty tries, Héritier made it. The two friends looked at each other and beamed. Now they could enjoy a breakfast of soup, dried meat, vegetables, and hot chocolate.

But then, bad luck. The small fire went out.

"Perhaps we'd better save our matches and try again when the wind is quieter," Berclaz said.

Héritier nodded. He leaned over to raise the rucksack so he could put the stove back in it. But he leaned over just a few inches too far, and began to lose his balance. Berclaz quickly grabbed his friend's arm to keep him from going over the edge. He kept Héritier from sliding off. But the sudden movement caused the small stove to

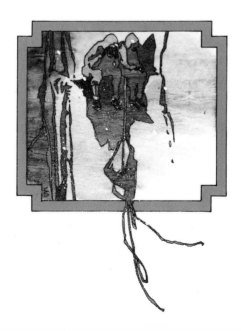

30

tumble off Berclaz's lap and fall thousands of feet down the mountainside.

"I think we'll have to wait a little longer for a warm meal," Héritier murmured sadly.

The two friends were going to wait much longer than they thought. The storm continued. They lasted another day, another night, and another morning. But they had become very tired and low in spirits.

A tiny ray of sun broke though the heavy clouds on the afternoon of the third day. Berclaz and Héritier were too far gone to feel like cheering. They did not believe that bit of sunlight meant a real change in the weather.

But then they could see a small patch of the valley below. They also saw people down there. Berclaz and Héritier began to scream as loud as they could. Then clouds returned. They no longer could see the valley.

Now Berclaz and Héritier really felt lost. It seemed to them that all hope was gone.

At this time, though, the snowfall did start to let up. By evening it had stopped. Snow had remained on the rock face, however. This made climbing impossible. Berclaz and Héritier faced another night on the ledge, but now they felt a little more cheerful.

They continued to take care of themselves. They still had enough food for a small dinner that night and a tiny breakfast the next morning. And at least they didn't have to worry about any more snow collecting on the ledge. When they took their short turns sleeping that night, they got more rest.

Héritier was sleeping and Berclaz was watching as dawn broke on the fourth day. Suddenly, Héritier sat up with a start. He put a finger on his lips, calling for silence. He seemed to be trying to hear something, and Berclaz wondered if Héritier might be dreaming. But suddenly Berclaz himself heard the faint sound of a motor. He sat up straight, hoping he heard right. It had to be a helicopter looking for survivors of the storm. It *had* to be!

In a moment the men's hearts leaped for joy. A small helicopter came into view. And it seemed to be headed straight for the northeast wall of the Badile. Berclaz and Héritier had no way of knowing that their cries the afternoon before had been heard in the valley. Their voices had reached two people almost 5,000 feet below their ledge. They had given the alarm.

Berclaz and Héritier were overjoyed to see the helicopter only 200 feet from them. They waved their arms so hard that they almost fell off the ledge!

Siegfried Stangier was the helicopter's pilot.

Beat Perren rode with him. They had found the two men on the mountainside. But the pilot knew that he was going to have to fly awfully close to the rock to drop a rescue cable to which the men could attach themselves. The wind still blew hard. He could easily smash the helicopter into the wall and kill the two men inside the machine. Stangier decided to fly to a nearby village and make plans.

Berclaz and Héritier did not worry when they saw the helicopter fly away. They knew they had been found. They had faith that the helicopter would return.

CHAPTER 5

Ready to Go

Stangier set the helicopter down near a village about twenty miles from the Piz Badile. He and Perren bought food and clothing. They planned to let it down to Berclaz and Héritier in a bundle by cable. Perren also bought two walkie-talkies. One of these radios would be let down to the men on the ledge. Then Perren and Stangier could talk to them.

Perren and Stangier looked upon the idea of dropping food, clothing, and walkie-talkie as a tryout for the rescue of the two men. The bundle holding these things would be snapped onto a carabiner at the end of a cable. Stangier would try to fly the helicopter to the right spot for the wind to carry the cable as close to the men as possible. If he flew right above them, the wind would carry the cable away from them. In any case, they would only have a few seconds to grab the bundle and unsnap it from the carabiner, because the helicopter could not stay long in one spot.

The same cable holding the bundle would be let down for Berclaz and Héritier. Each would attach the carabiner to his climbing harness. But before each could do that, he would have to unfasten himself from the rope holding him to the mountain. For several seconds nothing would protect him from a fatal fall. Of course, each man would have to be rescued separately. The second one to be saved would be left alone on the ledge for a short time.

Stangier and Perren returned to the cliff face less than ninety minutes after they left it. Berclaz and Héritier were more than happy to see them again. The helicopter flew just 150 feet above the

trapped men. Stangier and Perren looked for the best spot from which to lower the bundle.

Stangier had to move the helicopter around for fifteen minutes before finding the right spot. Perren leaned far out of the machine. He directed Stangier, who could not see the men. The bundle came close to them. It dangled in space just five feet away.

Finally, the cable brushed against the rock face. Héritier grabbed it and unsnapped it from the carabiner. But he was not prepared for the bundle's weight, about twenty pounds. He let his right hand hold on to the rope for just a second while his left hand clutched at the bundle. Because of its weight, he almost dropped the bundle. And then he almost fell off the ledge trying to hang onto it.

The helicopter now moved away. Berclaz and Héritier were delighted to find the walkie-talkie in the bundle. They could now hear another human voice for the first time in four days.

"Are you all right?" were the first words Berclaz and Héritier heard over the walkie-talkie. "Please tell us who and how you are. My name is Siegfried Stangier and I am the pilot of the helicopter. I must know if you think you have enough strength left to be removed from the mountain by cable."

Berclaz and Héritier gave their names. They

joyfully told Stangier that they felt strong enough.

Stangier explained what would happen. Each man would have to be removed from the ledge separately. Stangier planned to fly the first man to be rescued back for medical help. He hoped, though, to take the second man off soon after the first. Right now he told the men to eat a light meal. They should be ready to be lifted off the mountain within forty-five minutes to an hour. In the meantime Stangier would go and refuel his helicopter.

Berclaz and Héritier enjoyed their lunch. They especially liked the hot tea the bundle held. They felt connected to the human race once more. The rescue operation would be very dangerous. But right then they didn't worry about it.

Below them, the clouds continued to thin out. Above them and around the ledge, they noted, the clouds began to thicken. This might hold up the rescue operation.

CHAPTER 6

The Nest Disappears

Berclaz and Héritier waited four or five hours. By the time the sky had cleared enough, sunset was only two hours away. Stangier would have to move quickly if he were to remove the men before darkness made that impossible. Clouds were drifting across the Badile's top every few minutes. Stangier was prepared to fly around and around the mountain waiting for the top to be clear. He would always have to pay attention to the clouds. He would also have to allow for the high wind. If he was not careful, the wind might smash the helicopter against the rock.

The two men on the ledge flipped a coin to decide which one should be rescued first. Berclaz won. Héritier envied his friend. But he also knew that Berclaz would be the first one to take the big risk in this dangerous task. Héritier knew too, though, that as the second man, he would be taking a greater risk. After Berclaz left, Héritier

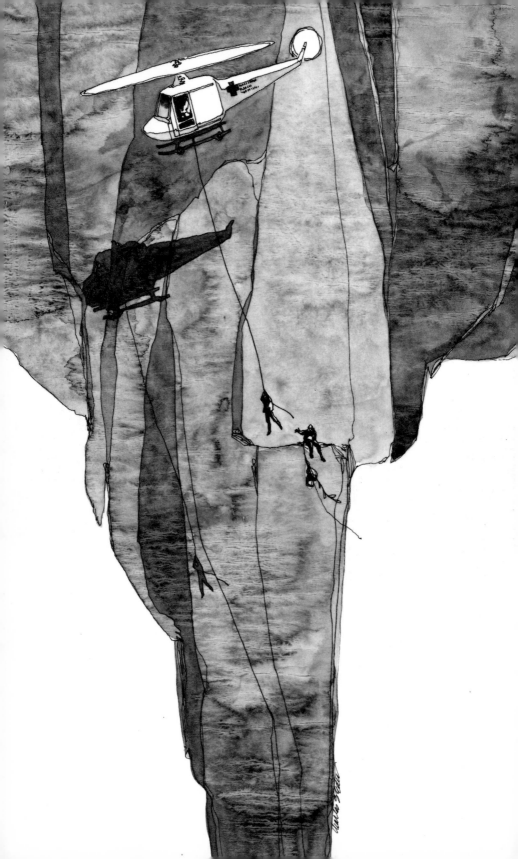

would have no one to hang on to before snapping the cable's carabiner to his harness.

As Stangier neared the mountain, the sky was clear. Again Perren leaned far out of the plane to direct the pilot to the best spot from which to drop the cable. Fortunately the wind went quiet for a few minutes. Stangier was able to guide the helicopter to the right place. It was 100 feet above the men and 30 feet away from the ledge. Only a minute had passed since the helicopter's return. The cable was already being lowered toward the ledge.

Berclaz unsnapped himself from the rope attached to the rock. He remained seated on the edge of the ledge. He put his left arm around Héritier's shoulder. Then he took one of Héritier's wrists in his right hand. When the cable came down, Héritier reached out for it. He almost had it when the helicopter backed off a few feet. The cable went with it.

In a minute the plane returned. Stangier awaited the feeling of extra weight on the cable. This would lower the helicopter several yards and tell him that Berclaz was as the cable's end.

Héritier watched the cable returning a foot or two away from the ledge. Again he reached out for it. The cable, swaying slightly in the wind, fell right against the palm of his hand. Héritier grabbed it and moved it a foot, over to the ring on

Berclaz's harness. Then Berclaz held the cable while Héritier tried to open the carabiner at the end to attach to his friend's harness. But with his numb fingers it was hard for Héritier to complete the task.

Again the cable suddenly rose, as the helicopter started to bob up and down in an unexpected gust of wind. The movement took Berclaz by surprise. He did not let go of the cable quickly

enough. Without being attached to the cable he was taken into the air with it. He clung to it with all his strength. He knew he had no choice. He let go of the cable with one hand so he could set the carabiner. He wouldn't let himself think about the thousands of feet that now separated him from earth.

Finally, after what seemed like hours, his hand found the carabiner and opened it. Somehow Berclaz managed to lower himself a few inches with his left hand without losing his grip. With his right hand he snapped the ring on his harness to the carabiner. Suddenly, the adventure of the last four days was over for Berclaz. He was safe. He swung from the cable as the helicopter returned to the valley. He prayed that Héritier would have the same luck.

But another spell of waiting still remained for Héritier. Thick clouds again returned to cover the area. These clouds pressed against the rock like a thick damp cloth.

Héritier was stuck on the mountain for another night, alone this time. At least he had enough food and warm clothing.

But getting through the night would be hard. Héritier had to keep himself awake. But he had no one to help him. Time passed much more slowly than it had before.

A few hours before dawn, Héritier saw a few stars. The sky might be clearing he thought. He did not want to fill himself with false hope, though. He counted the stars in a sort of game to keep himself awake.

Just before daybreak, thousands of stars appeared. The morning sky was clear!

The sun had just come up when Héritier heard the helicopter approaching. Again Stangier flew the machine up over the ledge. Perren dropped the cable down toward Héritier. But this time Stangier had trouble placing the helicopter in the right place for the drop. Time after time he thought that he had the perfect spot. But the cable always ended up a few feet from Héritier's grasp. Héritier could not understand what the trouble was. And he felt in great danger.

Héritier had already unsnapped himself from

the rope attaching him to the rock. Nothing protected him from a fatal fall except his own skill and clear thinking. He was in danger, but he could not allow fear to get the better of him. He waited patiently for the cable to fall within his arm's reach. He would not reach out for it unless he was sure he could do so safely. He knew how easy it would be for him to slide over the icy ledge if he lunged slightly forward.

Finally the cable fell right into Héritier's lap! He had only a few seconds to work. Héritier forced the carabiner open and linked his harness ring to it. Héritier continued to sit on the ledge until the helicopter lifted off. Then he fell a few feet into space before the cable brought him up short.

Héritier turned his head around to take a last look at the ledge. He squinted and peered at the mountainside. He searched for the rucksacks he and Berclaz had left behind. But already he could not find that tiny lip of rock on the great cliff face.

All that Héritier could see now was the entire northeast wall. It looked like a sheet of sheer solid rock. There seemed no place for a foothold or handhold.

Just forbidding and unyielding rock.